S0-AKS-719

ZEN IN THE ART OF
FLOWER ARRANGEMENT

ZEN
IN THE ART OF
FLOWER ARRANGEMENT

by
GUSTIE L. HERRIGEL

*An Introduction to the Spirit of
the Japanese Art of Flower Arrangement
With a Foreword by*
DAISETZ T. SUZUKI

Translated from the German by
R. F. C. HULL

ROUTLEDGE & KEGAN PAUL
London, Boston and Henley

First published in 1958
by Routledge & Kegan Paul Ltd
39 Store Street
London WC1E 7DD,
Broadway House, Newtown Road
Henley-on-Thames
Oxon RG9 1EN and
9 Park Street,
Boston, Mass. 02108, USA
Second Impression 1960
Reprinted and first published as a paperback 1974
Reprinted in 1979

Printed in Great Britain by
Unwin Brothers Limited, The Gresham Press, Old Woking, Surrey
A member of the Staples Printing Group

© Routledge & Kegan Paul Ltd 1958
Translated from the German by R. F. C. Hull
No part of this book may be reproduced in
any form without permission from the
publisher, except for the quotation of brief
passages in criticism

ISBN 0 7100 7941 9 (c)
ISBN 0 7100 7942 7 (p)

嵯峨

生花の道

風韻

九十翁 毛雲

The Wonderful Art of Flower Arrangement

TABLE OF CONTENTS

Table of Contents

Some of the illustrations in the text are copied from photographs and sketches which I made myself, others are derived from Japanese booklets of the Tokugawa period and from drawings by the Master, Bokuyo Takeda. The Japanese characters on the cover and title page were written by the 91-year-old Dr. Jun Komachiya.

FOREWORD

Daisetz T. Suzuki

I N EVERY artistic endeavour there comes a moment when one has to make oneself conscious of the two aspects of the art: the metaphysical and the practical, the supra-rational and the rational, or, to borrow an expression from Indian philosophy, the *prajna* and *vijnana* aspects. The practical, rational, *vijnana* aspect of painting is the handling of the brush, the mixing of colours, the drawing of lines; in short, its technique.

Yet mastery of technique alone does not satisfy; we feel in the depths of our consciousness that there is something more to be reached and to be discovered. Teaching and learning are not enough, they do not help us to penetrate the mystery of art; and so long as we have not experienced this mystery, no art is real art. The mystery belongs to the realm of metaphysics, is beyond rationality; it springs from *prajna*, transcendental wisdom. The Western mind has been coarsened by the techniques of exact analysis, whereas the Eastern mind is pre-eminently mystical and concerns itself with the so-called mystery of existence.

In a certain sense life is art. However long or short life may be, no matter under what conditions we have to live it, we all want to make the best of it— the best not only in the technique of living, but also in understanding its meaning. But that implies apprehending a glimmer of its mystery. From this standpoint the Japanese consider every art to be a form of schooling which grants insight into life's beauty, for beauty transcends all rationality and utility thinking, it is the mystery itself. In this sense Zen has close affinities with the arts, with painting, tea drinking, flower arrangement, fencing, archery, and suchlike.

The late Professor Eugen Herrigel's little book, *Zen in the Art of Archery*, is still causing powerful reactions among American scholars. In a recently published broadcast lecture on 'The Secret of Zen', Professor Gilbert Highet of Columbia University says: 'Some years ago a publisher sent me a little book to glance through'. This was none other than Herrigel's book. But he thought at the time: 'What could be more remote from my own life and that of my friends than Zen Buddhism and Japanese archery?' So he laid the book aside. Yet evidently there was something about it that he 'could not forget'. Later he made another attempt to read it. 'This time it seemed to me even stranger than before, even more unforgettable. It began to link up with other interests of mine, with something I had read about the Japanese art of flower arrangement. When, later, I wrote an essay on Japanese *haiku* poetry, still other connecting links began to grow.'

After he had finally read the book to the end and found out something about Zen Buddhism and archery, Professor Highet turned to Mrs. Herrigel. 'Herrigel's wife', he said, 'has acquired mastery in two of the loveliest Japanese arts, painting and flower arrangement.' He added in brackets: 'I wish somebody could persuade her to write a similar book on "Zen in the Art of Flower Arrangement". It would be of even greater interest.' While this American critic was expressing the wish that Mrs. Herrigel might write a counterpart to her husband's book, she had already fulfilled it.

Art is studied in Japan not only for art's sake, but for spiritual enlightenment. If art stops short at art and does not lead to something deeper and more fundamental, if, that is to say, art does not become equivalent to something spiritual, the Japanese would not consider it worth learning. Art and religion are closely bound up with one another in the history of Japanese culture. The art of flower arrangement is not, in its truest sense, an art, but rather the expression of a much deeper experience of life. The flowers should be arranged in such a way that we are reminded of the lilies of the field, whose beauty was not surpassed by Solomon in all his glory. Even the modest wild flower, named *nazuna*, was regarded with reverence by Basho, the Japanese *haiku* poet of the seventeenth century. For it proclaims the deepest secret of Nature, which is an artless art'.

I hope the reader will be touched by the breath of the spirit when he reads this book.

ZEN IN THE ART OF
FLOWER ARRANGEMENT

INTRODUCTORY

Soon after our return from Japan in the late summer of 1930, where I had spent six years while my husband was teaching at Tohoku University in Sendai, I received repeated requests that I should say something about the Japanese art of flower arrangement. For a long time I could not make up my mind to do this. The reason for my hesitation lay, above all, in the reverence which honours 'silence' as a positive source of strength no less than the experience one has gained in the realm of not-knowing. Since the 'real truth' can, ultimately, only be written about but never directly expressed, it may seem a paradoxical undertaking to try to clothe the 'Flowers' Way' in words. My silence was further strengthened by the reflection that, because of the exotic and therefore alluring strangeness of this domain, the interest aroused in it might perhaps be due not so much to a wish to penetrate, with patience and perseverance, into the deeper meaning of the teaching, but rather to sensational curiosity.

Nevertheless, renewed requests continued to reach me, which afforded proof of serious interest. So I came to a decision after all, and have made an attempt to say something about the spirit of Japanese flower arrangement, to fix in simple words the mysterious and ultimately inexpressible thing about this art. Anyone who lives quite naturally in this tradition will have neither need nor cause to give a rational account of his knowledge and experience. That is why no attempt has so far been made to write about the deeper meaning and spirit of this art. Another reason for this lies in the fact that the few old texts which might give us a clue are written in such a way as to be very difficult to decipher and to interpret.

Also, there are probably not many foreigners who have had the opportunity of receiving such a long training from teachers of the old tradition, and consequently of forming an opinion on the basis of their own experience as well as of personal tuition. Here I may perhaps mention that, through pro-longed study, I was permitted to learn this art well enough to take a Master's Degree in the year 1929, in the public examinations held under the Master Bokuyo Takeda.

According to ancient custom, the Master solemnly handed me a black gown on which his coat of arms was emblazoned in white. The honorific title of 'Waxing Moon' was bestowed upon me in a diploma elegantly brushed in ink. The trunk containing the diary I kept in Japan was unfortunately lost later in Germany, together with all my other belongings. So I shall try to live everything over again, without notes.

THE INSTRUCTION

THE SALUTATION

SINCE, FOR linguistic reasons alone, I had to take private lessons anyway, the Master Bokuyo Takeda volunteered to give them to me. Thus he came one afternoon to tea, accompanied by the assistant of the Botanical Institute of the University, who spoke English fluently. The private lessons thus inaugurated in our house were a special favour, so that my husband could be present too. Sometimes the psychologist Dr. Chiba, and a Dr. Aono, were there as well. The lessons took place in our European sitting-room. Sitting for hours on flat cushions, as is customary in Japan, would have been too much of a strain for us.

So this was the celebrated Master Bokuyo Takeda: a tall gentleman in a plain silk kimono with the usual short upper garment, bearing on the sleeves the coat of arms of his family. In his hand he held a simple yet impressively painted fan. After many

4

official obeisances and words of salutation, we took our places. The Master amiably sat with us at the high table, so that we did not need to sit on low cushions. At the right moment the 'boy', mindful of good manners, brought in the steaming wet towels in a bamboo basket, which are so pleasant for wiping the face and hands in hot weather. Then a very refreshing tea, called 'ban-cha', was drunk out of finely-painted bowls, and the usual sikishima cigarettes were smoked.

After this introductory refreshment, conversation started. The Master was very friendly, telling us all sorts of interesting things in his lively, convincing manner. Finally, to crown all, he gave an unsurpassed *Noh* recitation; for in this field too he was an enthusiastic connoisseur. Yet he was recognized not only as an artist, but as a worthy representative of fine manners. He attached especial importance to the moulding of character and the 'heart', to cleanliness, modesty and honesty in everyday dealings. The question of fees was not discussed, as it is customary to arrange this only at the end of the year. The fee is handed over in a special envelope, tastefully tied, together with the bills. It is magnanimously left to the pupil himself to give according to his capacities.

The Instruction

The lessons began a few days after the Master's first visit. The Master had sent me beforehand everything I would need.

So there the tall willow branches lay, tied together in an oblong container. A natural-coloured bamboo vase stood ready on a black lacquer stand. A strong pair of pruning shears, rather clumsy to my way of thinking, a small saw, a hemmed cloth of unbleached cotton for keeping the things clean, all lay in their places. Not forgetting a small can of water for freshening and watering the plants once they were 'set'.

Carefully the bast that held the bundle together was untied, without using the shears. No pulling or cutting, no impatience, no disorder. The bast was carefully rolled round the finger and laid on a tablet. Everything was done in a timeless silence, every move of the hand was executed precisely and soundlessly. Concentration on the real work had already begun.

A Y-shaped fork is cut from pliable wood to give support to the branches that are to stand in the vase. This piece of wood, cut according to the thickness of the branches, and called a *kubari*, is inserted into

6

the mouth of the vase, about one to two centimetres deep.

Now follows a contemplative examination of the loose branches. Each one is lovingly examined and tested for its pliability and natural 'bent'. Thus there

arises before the Master's eye the image that is to be put together. Then the first branch is carefully felt all over, tested here and there for suppleness, in order to find out how it can be brought with the least effort and most sparingly into the form it is intended to represent. At this point it is important to consider which of the three main branches it should embody, and which should be the 'light' side and the 'shadow' side. Much depends on your being able to feel how the branch accommodates itself most willingly, thus entering into a relationship of inner tension with it.

Its elasticity varies; only when you have done everything correctly will the branch, quite effortlessly and without subsequent correction, acquire its form, as if it had grown like that by itself. A fair amount of practice is needed before you get the right feeling and realize that this shaping is an exceeding subtle art. Thus, with a stroking movement and slow, light pressure at various points, a branch is bent into the right shape, or shortened and trimmed. One might think the plant must suffer no pain, so carefully is it handled, until it finally keeps the desired form.

To begin with only the three main branches are arranged, consisting of a tall one, a shorter one, and a low one. The points of the twigs should together form a triangle. If they are arranged in the right way, the three branches have the effect of a single branch unfolding in different directions.

After filling the vase with water, it is placed on a large stand in a quiet, open, and worthy part of the room. This, in a Japanese house, is the *tokonoma*, a specially built wall niche.

The task for next time is then given, and everything is cleared away. So ends the first lesson. Another sip of hot tea, a sikishima, and obeisances.

Strange and disconcerting it was that this first

Basic Forms of the Schema

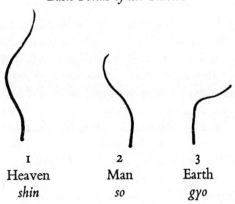

1	2	3
Heaven	Man	Earth
shin	*so*	*gyo*

Optional Right and Left Basic Forms

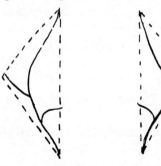

1	2
right-sided:	left-sided:
hon doko	*gyaku doko*
Earth on the right	Earth on the left

9

lesson passed almost wordlessly, without any preparatory introduction, and my questions were not taken as important. It was already apparent that more emphasis is laid on wordless, silent understanding and communication. For long stretches the interpreter had to be content with the role of spectator. But he was needed when the Book of Rules was handed over, for translating the interesting characters in this venerable document.

The task for the next lesson consisted in arranging three branches along similar lines, so that they stood firm in the *kubari* as if growing out of one stem, and kept their balance in the tall vase. For this one could take apart the branches already found suitable by the Master and try to put them together again in the same position—in other words, copy them. But fresh branches might also be put together for a new vase, following the Master's model.

With the devouring glance of a beginner I had watched and followed the proceedings during the first lesson. How simple and easy it all seemed! In a few lessons, I thought, I would be able to master everything, especially as arranging flowers in vases had always been my favourite occupation, and the will for artistic creation was not lacking.

Yet when I joyfully began shaping and securing

the wooden fork, it soon became clear that this work would need time and patience, as also the setting and balancing of the tall branches. After much assiduous experimenting and practising, I looked forward to the next lesson with satisfied pride. The filled bamboo vase stood there in all its glory!

THE SECOND LESSON

The Master brought with him some beautifully bound volumes of fine paper, wonderfully suited to brush-and-ink paintings. Thus it came about that at the end of each lesson little masterpieces had taken shape, exact replicas of the newly arranged flower-pieces. The name of the plant was added at the side in flowery calligraphy.

This time too, as always, refreshing tea was drunk. Only after very amiable words had been exchanged did the time come to turn one's attention to the branches. With a friendly, unmoved expression of face, the Master carried out his examination. Then, without much explanation, he very politely took the branches out of the vase. This meant that my performance was in no way satisfactory. Thereupon the Master put the branches, freshly arranged, back in their container.

The Instruction

At first I was taken aback, for this procedure seemed to me very odd. Yet, with the intention of getting at the roots of the process, I acquiesced, even though shaking my head. This inexplicable way of doing things seemed to contradict the Master's much emphasized politeness. Why couldn't he adjust himself in this matter, too, to the psyche of the European, who does not assume from the start that he can do nothing?

Meanwhile the gardener had brought in some fresh willows. After they had been set in position and painted, we took farewell till next time over tea and sikishimas. How quickly such a lesson passed!

THE THIRD LESSON

Sedulously I practised for the next lesson. The procedure last time was not going to be repeated. Yet even in the lessons that followed, personal idiosyncrasies and originality in making new experiments met with little recognition. The Master's firmness, his evident superiority, put one's own thoughts and actions more and more in question. Had one to become quite small and reach the zero of one's being?

In the next lessons the thing was to watch closely

and see where the secret of success might lie. Already another lesson was over. The clock hardly played any role: sometimes the time allowed for practice was longer, sometimes shorter.

To begin with, the work resembled outward imitation, or an activity more or less governed by the will. From the centre, from inside, nothing happened. The question as to how one might attain this inwardness met with the seemingly monotonous reply: only by copying the models as often and as faithfully as possible. I could not make much of this advice, although I believed it. Nevertheless the lessons were not in the least monotonous; always there were new branches and leaves and the play of light and shadow. Willows are very suitable for a beginner, as they are easy to shape and particularly attractive in their dress of catkins. But large-leaved plants too, such as aspidistra and *Rhodea japonica*, are grateful to work with and, although all green, are in no way monotonous or dull in their effects if attention is paid to their veining and the light and shadow side.

Time and again one can see how variously the basic 'Principle of Three' can be differentiated and modulated.

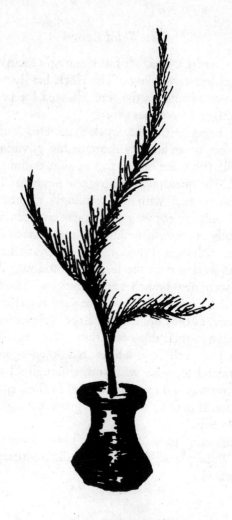

Genista (*enishida*) Broom
Three-piece *seikwa*

RESULT OF FURTHER LESSONS

The lessons passed silently, for in the East especial value has always been laid on 'silent' communication, or more precisely, on communication 'from heart to heart'. It was thought that only through personal transmission could the spirit of the teaching be protected from dogmatic rigidity. On the other hand, care was taken that the rules sacred to the Master, and the experiences he had so toilsomely acquired, should not come to the knowledge of unqualified persons. It was also considered a bold undertaking to try to put the real meaning into words. The original way of communication was therefore called the 'secret way'. The teaching went father to son, from teacher to favourite pupil. The first requisite for this was a spiritual affinity between the two, and above all the proven ability of the pupil to grasp his Master's teaching intuitively.

This is the essential reason why there are comparatively few texts on the art of flower arrangement, and why they limit themselves either to illustrations or to practical hints. Mostly they summarize only the instructions to be followed at the flower ceremony. They hardly breathe a word about the deep, secret meaning of these instructions. Even the Books of Rules claim only that the 'true' teaching of the long dead Masters can be recognized and experienced anew in the present Master. Very little is said about the real teaching itself. Thus, behind the communication 'from heart to heart', there is the hidden intention of not simply letting the pupil learn a definite body of doctrine by rote, of not handing on to him ready-made knowledge and clever tricks, but of arousing in him the duty of discovering the spirit of flower arrangement through his own experience.

This explains why a good teacher will repeatedly reject his pupils' work, often without giving any adequate reason. For the real content of the teaching reveals itself only to those who are capable of experiencing it and who know how to grasp it as soon as it offers itself to them. The 'true spirit' of the teaching cannot be formulated in words. Words are at best only bridges to it. For it has been written: 'He who talks, does not know; he who knows, does not talk' (Lao-Tzu). Hence the Master must often limit himself to making an exemplary model under the pupil's eyes. It is the task of the pupil to learn from this what it ultimately depends on, and, from what he sees, to push forward into the Invisible that underlies the visible.

Result of Further Lessons

Through years of practice, the pupil may get far enough to awaken in himself an attitude of mind capable of achievements that can endure in every respect. But even quite primitive efforts, so long as they have the power to communicate something 'archetypal', are accepted and praised by the Master. Only technically correct constructions, which are nothing more than that, leave one unrelated and cold. They have a dead effect.

The Master follows this method of instruction with the intention of communicating the 'living spirit' of the teaching to his pupils, so that they can gradually grow into that spiritual atmosphere in which the original, creative experience can flourish and mature.

This was the way in which the Master Bokuyo Takeda worked.

Thus, for a period of years, he came every week to our house by the Hirose River, between the tall camellia bushes and the cherry trees. How pleasant it was to see the composure, the unencumbered ease of movement, with which a new structure took shape under his hands, in an unbroken rhythm of nature, life, and art. Not just part of a plant, but an exquisite, organically grown whole was there for our contemplation at the end of the lesson.

The Instruction

Sometimes the plants rocked as if swaying in the wind, or like people moving in a fluent, serene dance. Or they stood as if battered by the tempest, or festively clad according to the season, pulsing in every limb with the spring, or tinted in glowing colours by the autumn.

But the example of the Master's humanity was just as effective as his work and gave the lessons a special meaning. Never did the Master omit the spoken or unspoken admonishment to cultivate the right attitude to the world with ever increasing mindfulness. And since he himself lived according to this rule, he was convincing.

The summons to mindfulness is more important than zealous enthusiasm. Nor is it sufficient to set about one's work as though one were going to five o'clock tea. Arranging flowers is no pastime and is not intended for distraction. You must collect yourself beforehand and begin early in the morning by performing all your activities without fuss, without haste, and giving them the expression of inner balance and harmony. This attitude should become so natural that it turns into a secure possession. One can well say that the 'inner work' of flower arrangement must keep pace with the outer. Only so can it be a wholeness of heaven, man, and earth. The hour for arranging the flowers pervades the entire day, it does not stand outside. But it is not easy to go the modest way of the flowers from morning till evening!

The Master observes everything, nothing escapes him. His observations serve him as a guide in setting further tasks. Slowly he passes on to the arranging of five, seven, nine branches, granting greater freedom if no misuse is to be feared.

Working in such a modulation of colours and branches can be very exciting. But the essential thing is always the 'Principle of Three' as the measure and midpoint of the structure, of the experience and the inner vision. That is why the practice of this art is not finished even after many years. The astonished question of foreigners: 'What, still at it?' testifies to a superficiality of viewpoint. The good pupil understands in the end: the longer the better. In this school there is no 'finishing' in our sense. Even the setting of only three branches, apparently the easiest thing, can, if justice is done to the 'universal heart', be very difficult.

The advanced pupil understands this and sees it embodied before him in the flower exhibitions that often take place. Even here the Master will not exhibit a conspicuous work of art, but, perhaps in a quite simple bowl, he will arrange a small twig covered with tree lichen, a few blades of grass, some stalks, a little moss. With the simplest means he achieves a natural structure that convinces by its mere presence and speaks for itself, although it does not woo for recognition with alluring colours. The suggestive Japanese word *shibumi*, which can be translated according to sense as 'genuine', 'true', 'simple', 'chaste', 'noble', befits him and his art. Hence his honorific title: Bokuyo, the Simple, Chaste One.

FLOWER EXHIBITIONS

Flower exhibitions were organized by the Master at the end of each yearly course. All the girls sent in contributions. In a large room—maybe a tea house —they were arranged in tiers. An oblong wooden tablet rested against each vase, on which the name of the pupil could be read. The Master too sent in a contribution, hidden somewhere among the others, not placed right in the front row. And what he had contributed was, as I said, so inconspicuous that it hardly drew any attention to itself. But had you discovered it, you could not have escaped the impression it made.

Begonia evansiana (*shiukaido*)
Three stems of begonia with well-distributed leaves. This
moderate, middle form is known simply as *seikwa*

It is natural that, as a European, one should look forward to the first lessons in flower arrangement with uninhibited eagerness to perform great feats and with a feeling of self-confidence. And indeed, besides skilful hands and artistic taste, cannot these qualities be regarded as especially desirable assets? Yet even at the first lessons the beginner who thinks like that is overcome by a sense of perplexity. He finds that he is unable to get into closer contact with this art, and has no inner relationship to the points where it starts from. If he wants to penetrate to its roots, he will be forced to decide whether he was attracted only by the artistic and aesthetic elements, or whether he seeks to experience the all-embracing, total nature of this art. In the latter case he will have to admit, again and again, that he must begin like a child, that any sort of ambition is a hindrance, and that any desire for personal uniqueness stands in the way of development. That, quite small and modest, he must look away from his ego in order to work as quietly and selflessly as this Eastern attitude demands. At first the whole centre of gravity seems to lie in this preparatory attitude. For whatever one does as a beginner will appear wrong in the eyes of the Master if this first and last requisite is missing. The Master has seen, from the example of himself and others, how fuss, haste and impatience only bring discord into his life and his surroundings. He has listened to the plants in the wind and the storm, seen how they yield, bending and swaying, how they calmly let everything pass over their heads and so remain uninjured.

As I have already mentioned, the performance itself is of secondary importance compared with the inner attitude. To the degree that the pupil can summon up courage for the necessary self-discipline and this keeps pace with his artistic ability, he will find, not only as an artist but also as a human being, a special relationship to his performance, to this quiet, unswerving creation out of inner harmony. To begin with the European finds it difficult to understand why he should fit himself into a pattern and only then work free of it. But bit by bit he begins to realize, and perhaps also to experience, that this 'fitting in' is actually a springboard for true creativity. I can best explain this by means of an illustration: only when a swimmer finds himself in playful control of his technique can he let himself be borne by the water.

An advanced pupil, however, will never be content with merely copying the art or peculiarities of his Master. The knowledge and increasing development that are required can be neither mechanically imitated nor experienced second-hand. For the pattern, which at first appears merely as an outward form, becomes the inner form of flower arrangement as soon as the rules enter into life itself.

Everything that began by seeming affected and unclear becomes self-evident as soon as the bud unfolds in the maturing pupil. Even the rules find their fulfilment in everyday life as a voluntary adaptation to the demands which each day brings. Thus the moulding and realization of one's own nature goes hand in hand with the creativeness that comes to expression in this flowery 'gentle' art. The actual technique is not so very difficult, and it is not the decisive thing. Dexterity comes of its own accord through the many tests which the pupil has to pass. The relaxed yet suspenseful attitude, however, is rather to be compared with the dreamy playing of a child, the devotion of a believer, or the intuitive vision of an artist.

COMMUNAL INSTRUCTION

The place I want to tell about now lay in the centre of the university town of Sendai, a bare half-hour from the sea, near one of the loveliest of Japan's thousand pine-covered islands, named *matsushima*. There, surrounded by a well-kept garden, stood a house built in old Japanese style. It was the house of the Master Bokuyo Takeda, the house in which he held his famed courses of instruction. Beginners as well as advanced pupils, both girls and men, could attend these in a large room. Here, for many years past, the Master had stood most days of the week, from early morning till late evening, at the disposal of countless eager pupils.

The number of girl students far exceeded that of the men, although the art of flowers was originally practised by men and for centuries was held in high esteem by the samurai. Later this changed, because every Japanese girl was expected to know how to arrange flowers. It was and still is part of the duties of a married woman to decorate the family's living-rooms. Nor, as I discovered in the meantime, has the need to keep up this graceful custom in any way diminished since the end of the Second World War, but has on the contrary strengthened and increased. Masters, now as then, visit the rooms of well-cared-for houses and give an opinion on the way the housewife decorates the *tokonoma* with flowers. Even large concerns, banks and factories

Picea jezoensis (*yezo–matsu*) Spruce
Seven-piece *seikwa*

nowadays give their employees the opportunity to devote themselves in a leisure hour, with the help of trained teachers, to this noble art, and to cultivate it, thereby collecting their strength and relaxing at the same time.

At the Master's house each girl student could choose her own day and hour in accordance with her domestic and other duties. There were girls and married women of all ages, from about 16 onwards, and one could be sure of meeting ten to fifteen of them at any hour of the day. The fee was so moderate that anyone could afford to attend these lessons. On the thick straw mats that covered the floor the coming and going was as soundless as the work itself. Many of the girls attended these lessons for years, so as to penetrate ever more deeply into the ultimate secrets of this difficult and yet so gentle art. When a girl entered the room she at once knelt down, supporting herself on her outstretched hands and bowing so low before the Master that she almost touched the floor with her forehead. With a second, equally deep bow she greeted the others present, then betook herself to a free place and sat down with her legs beneath her, Japanese fashion, on a thin cushion. In front of her, on a square black-lacquered board, she placed a vase of bamboo or metal—generally her own property—depending on the kind of branches or flowers to be used, which lay tied together beside the vase.

Carefully she untied the bundle, thoughtfully examining the branches or flowers until she had found the ones that seemed most suitable to her, and began to give them the form they would have to assume according to their role in the total picture. Sunk deep in herself, she sought to attain that state of mind in which it is possible to become one with the heart of the flower; for she knows from long experience and practice that this is not just a figure of speech. For only when this union of her own heart with the flower's heart—and indeed with the 'universal heart', as the Japanese Masters so felicitously express it—is truly established, does she rest in that unmoved stillness from which creation proceeds as if of itself, entirely unpurposingly. In her work is reflected, visible in the flesh to the expert eye of the Master, whether this union has been attained and is not just a deceptive illusion. The masklike face which the Japanese woman often puts on for show becomes, in that state of union, suddenly alive, actually quite beautiful and as if illuminated from within.

When a pupil thinks she has solved a task, she

hands over her vase to the Master. Between times, however, the Master himself makes the rounds, now and then pausing to inspect and pass an opinion. He examines the proffered vase, generally in silence, rejecting the whole thing with a movement of the hand or taking it apart, improving certain components and putting it together again. The pupil thanks him with a bow, carries the vase back to her place and studies it intently, in order to find out where she could have gone wrong. If she thinks she has discovered where the fault lay, she takes new branches and starts afresh; or she takes the model apart and puts it together again if there are no fresh branches at her disposal. Not until the Master consents does she leave the practice-room.

Some of the participants, particularly the younger ones, make a remarkable discovery. At first they feel that the presence of so many fellow students is a disturbance and follow every movement, if only out of the corner of an eye, or they let themselves be distracted by the shimmering colours of the kimonos. Although all unnecessary noise is avoided, and the plants and implements are handled almost soundlessly, yet one's interest in the way the others do their work can be distracting. Only gradually do you accustom yourself to feeling that all this is unimportant and undisturbing, and you discover to your satisfaction that the more your concentration is focused on the task the more deeply it can strike root. Even a loud noise penetrating into the practice room from outside is not noticed. Thus you find, as the indispensable precondition for this and probably every other Japanese art, that you must rest in unbroken stillness. And further, that this is actually realizable if you summon the strength to practise daily and do not let yourself be discouraged by failures.

Daily concentration, be it only for half an hour, builds the best counter-balance to the fraying tempo of everyday life and to that busy-mindedness which, instead of gathering together, only distracts. You see how much time you have only when you stop thinking that you have none.

BASIC RULES

The staying power needed for lifelong practice and obligatory study is probably the hardest thing of all. One could manage in a fairly short time to learn the traditional forms of Japanese flower arrangement by heart or to copy them mechanically. But anyone who takes it seriously, discovers that the art

Camellia (*tsubaki*)
Five-piece *seikwa* in Cloisonné vase

of flowers evokes and requires a slow inward transformation and maturation. Only then can one go the 'flowers' way'. Everything else is contingent on this requirement. It may be that this attitude seems very naive, and is therefore easily overlooked. Also, people are apt to form a vague idea of this activity and to turn their whole attention to the various possibilities which they want to learn and master, on the assumption that the rest will come of its own accord. Nothing could be more mistaken. Anyone who has skilled fingers and the necessary interest in form can master the technique outwardly. But the further you advance the more you come to realize how much depends on taking the central precepts seriously, and that you can create nothing 'whole' unless these 'naive' requirements are per-severingly followed. It is one of the peculiarities of the Far East to begin with something small and unassuming; nothing is obvious, it has to be prac-tised over and over again until there are no more half measures, until it becomes one's very own. The first steps are the hardest. Anyone who fails there, remains stuck. So there is nothing for it but to begin quite unpretentiously. It is no easy schooling, not a finger exercise, but a school of experience. The technique should be assimilated, but not overestimated. Practising with the heart, harmonious wholeness of body, soul and surroundings are the important things. The presence of the Master makes it easier to find the 'true' harmonious attitude which is needed in order to understand the nature of the 'flowers' way' and to follow it correctly.

The 'Principle of Three' is important not only in handling the plants, but also in relating to one's fellows and the world of animals. The pupil will endeavour to do justice to every creature after its kind. He reaches this attitude intuitively; for the example and mere presence of the Master bring conviction and show the way. So understood by the practitioner and sensed by the observer, the idea of the Principle of Three is continually realized in new ways.

The symbolic language of the three branches is expressed by 'heaven', 'man', and 'earth'. It speaks to us not only from the outside. It is pervaded by the eternal rhythm of form and content, substance and emptiness. The beholder, 'man' himself, stands in the centre—perhaps he even receives a reflection of this eternity. Enriched by this experience, he can muster the perseverance and patience needed for schooling himself. He has recognized that looking away from himself leads to the great detachment

Aster tartaricus (*shion*)

Seikwa composed of three sprays, surrounded by five orna-
mental leaves, in simple porcelain vase on small stand

and composure, to 'inner collection' and 'stillness'. Convinced by the efficacy of this attitude, he will carry it beyond his practice hours into the smallest avocations and expressions of everyday life. He lives from the mid-point, which the Principle of Three exemplifies as the symbol of wholeness in flower arrangement: Man (*so*) stands in the middle position between Heaven (*shin*) and Earth (*gyo*).

THE MASTER

I N REMEMBRANCE of my revered Master Bokuyo Takeda I would like to let his words and teaching speak for themselves:

Man and plant are mortal and changeable; the meaning and essence of flower setting is eternal.

You should seek the outward form from inside.

It is unimportant what material is used. The right thought alone leads to God; offer sacrifice with this in mind.

Beauty coupled with virtue is powerful.

Beauty alone is of no avail; it perfects itself only in conjunction with 'true' sentiment.

Correct handling of flowers refines the personality.

Run your house with inner quietness, self-control and justice.

Do not be negligent in your household and profession.

The Principle of Three

Cultivate friendship with true and aristocratic feeling.

THE PRINCIPLE OF THREE

According to the Principle of Three, the universe can be divided into three realms, though at bottom it is one: heaven, earth, and the world of men.

The Principle of Three, which forms the basis of flower-setting, has its origin in Buddhism. It is a spiritual principle and has, as I have said, a cosmic significance. The idea of the number three in Buddhism migrated from India via China to Japan. Priestly progenitors of the flower cult fitted this triad, together with other more or less significant uneven numbers, into its basic structure as vehicles of religious thought. This articulation reflects the profound meaning of the cosmic law of growth. The starting-point of the three became, increasingly, the mid-point of a structure ramifying ultimately into art. In the Principle of Three one 'sets' oneself and at the same time not oneself—for flower-heart, man's heart and universal heart are one. Man lives in essential communion with the plant as with the whole universe. He is the channel for the spiritual as well as the earthly, and everything forms the unbroken Three-in-One.

In the cycle of the three man stands midway between heaven and earth. He is nourished by aerial roots and sustained by earthly roots. Thus he is simultaneously one with the universal heart and the primal 'Ground'. He lives from his own centre, which for him is just as much the world centre and the universal centre. Just as his unwilled individuality embodies the truth of heaven itself, so the power which makes the flowers grow is the same which guides the spiritual hand in flower-setting, and which is nourished directly from the universal heart. The true pupil is not turned away from the world in this art, still less does he escape from the world; rather, he lives in the centre of the universal process and accordingly stands in the world with both feet. He accepts it—whatever it may bring—as fate. Indeed, he is happy to live in the world and does not reject it. For him it is the frame in which his own being becomes reality.

The Principle of Three contains, in its unsymmetrical structure, the reciprocal action of fullness and emptiness, vitality and detachment; it encloses the whole cycle within it. In his work, the pupil gives the totality of heaven, man and earth a further 'unfolding' in visible unity and symbolic form. He implants into it the limitations of his ego and at the same time equalizes them. Since he participates with his whole being, the little ego becomes unimportant in the total cosmos; it makes way for the non-ego. The European from his standpoint might formulate this as follows: after the differentiations are surpassed, the way to one's real self is unfolded, and hence to wholeness. The pupil will then cling to the pattern no longer; he will forget the Principle of Three. It ceases to exist; the stepping-stones are forgotten so as to reach the everlasting origin.

FROM THE BOOK OF RULES

In a book of rules for memorizing, the rudiments of the inner and outer attitude required for arranging flowers are laid down:

Behave well in class and do not chatter.

It is unbecoming to behave as though one knew more than one does in reality; far better to act modestly.

Be proud of nothing; there are stages beyond the one you are on now.

If anyone is outwardly skilled in flower-arrangement, yet lacks artistic and human delicacy of feeling, he is nevertheless ignorant.

Whoever, through his way of arranging flowers,

Narcissus tarzetta (*suisen*)

Formal *seikwa*. Three stems with four leaves each, their apices
turned towards the flowers. The leaves were taken apart and
regrouped so that the taller ones are outside and the shorter
ones inside

can make a room beautiful with harmony and good taste, is to be called skilful, even if his way of arranging them is unskilful.

It is deemed a politeness not to execute any hasty movements.

Flowers should be handled tenderly.

Do not expect more from the flowers than their nature can bear.

Do not look down on other schools, but take from them whatever is good. Drop anything bad, even if it comes from your own school.

Superficiality always leads to perversity.

The Masters of old were true teachers. We should recognize them clearly again in the present teachers.

CONGRESS OF MASTERS

In the year 1928, Bokuyo Takeda invited the leading flower Masters of Japan to a congress at Sendai. Each of them was to give practical examples demonstrating his particular way of interpreting this art. Daily they began early in the morning, exhibited their work in choice vases, and until late in the evening there was an unabated stream of visitors who never grew tired of admiring, expertly and reverently, the astonishing variety of differentiated

Camellia *nageire*
Flower, bud and five leaves on a single stem, in polished pewter
vase

modulations of one and the same theme in masterly forms.

On the eighth day the Masters assembled for the last time. In their farewell speeches they regretted having to take the flowers out of their vases in the evening, so as to leave these free for the tasks of the following day. Because of this, the flowers were denied going their way to fulfilment. As living creatures their time was cut short, they could not perfect themselves to the point where maturity passes over into the peculiar beauty of fading. The Masters decided to commemorate the flowers by a solemn act, long in use, whereby the flowers are cut off, thrown away if faded, or, according to an earlier custom, carried away by the waves.

Amid general agreement it was decided to bury the flowers in Master Takeda's garden and to set up a commemorative tablet bearing on its front the inscription: 'To the souls of the sacrificed flowers', while on the back were carved the names of the Masters taking part. As I later discovered, my name was subsequently added.

COMMUNICATION OF THE TEACHING

Not only the spiritual content of the teaching, but technical experiences in particular, were kept strictly secret. These included the various methods of prolonging the life of plants. They were communicated only orally, if not by silent example, from teacher to pupil, as soon as he was mature enough to take over the office of teacher in succession to him.

This ban was broken only in the present. Thus my own Master, a representative of the Hongen-Enshju teaching, published a large, very graphic work in four volumes, with his own illustrations and explanations, on *Ikebana* (flower arrangement). As he himself related, great exception was taken at first to his having revealed so much to the public. But he replied that many of the old practices were out of date today and that it would not do the spirit of the teaching any harm if this or that were made known.

Yet, elaborately as he has discussed the teaching and the idea of flower arrangement, he was still not able to communicate it in such a way that it could be entirely comprehended by the intellect. Every exposition reaches its limits where the ultimate truth is concerned, where we can no longer say anything but can only experience it. It is true of every art that you cannot acquire what you have not felt.

This is particularly true of the arts of the Far

East, whether it be flower arrangement, painting, archery, or whatever else. For they all presuppose not only artistic endowment, but a spiritual attitude, acquired through many years of practice in concentration, which enables the pupil to experience that on which everything depends: the essentially inexpressible, the Absolute, the 'spirit' itself.

Although it is greatly to be welcomed that there is more and more of a need in present-day Japan to depart from the merely oral tradition and to make it accessible to the wider public, it should not be overlooked that the older method of instruction had an extraordinarily significant subsidiary effect. By keeping the teaching secret, the Japanese was educated to that peculiar reverence for all products of art which strikes the foreigner at every turn. One has only to observe how reverently a Japanese behaves at a flower exhibition, how he contemplates an ink-painting, or how he takes a valuable sword in his hand, as though, by immersing himself in the work of the creator, he could also partake of his spirit.

In keeping with this is the veneration which the Japanese feels for the *sensei*, his teacher; for it is he who gradually imparts to the pupil his most secret and deepest knowledge of the ultimate things, and thus transfers to him his spirit. Permeated by his high task, the teacher will be the best example for the pupil who knows how to appreciate human qualities no less than the capacity to expound knowledge. In the conduct of his life he realizes the meaning and the effect of his teaching; both as a man and an artist he sets upon it the seal of truth. Such immediate communication has evoked and implanted in the heart of the Japanese a reverence for the teaching which he has largely preserved to the present day.

The teacher is not just an 'instructor'. Everything that, by his conduct, serves to strengthen the pupil's human dignity, uprightness, tact and responsibility is as important and meaningful as the learning he imparts. Were this basic condition lacking, he would not be a 'true' teacher, not an all-round man worthy of belief. The pupil has an uncommonly sharp nose for how far the teacher fulfils his vocation. He sees in him the fatherly friend, the counsellor in whom he displays the utmost confidence and to whom he remains devoted and thankful for the rest of his life.

It is related of a certain prince that the first person he visited on a journey was his simple and venerable old teacher in his modest dwelling. Everybody stood

Hosta ovata (*giboshi*) Blue Day Lily
Carefully executed *seikwa* with broad leaves arranged serially,
in simple porcelain vase

ready to receive the noble gentleman with marks of respect. But the teacher knew that a good pupil would seek him out, and so he did right to await him in his own home. Here again it is evident how important is the human relationship between pupil and teacher. Thus the teacher, who was a living model for his pupil and gave him good advice and support on life's journey, always enjoys the fullest confidence and abiding esteem; he keeps his place in the pupil's heart.

THE TECHNIQUE

THE ART of flower arrangement is called in Japanese *ikebana*. *Hana* or *bana* means flower. *Ikebana* can be translated freely as 'keeping living plants alive in containers filled with water'. The word 'flower' in this context includes anything plant-like, such as twigs and branches, leaves of all kinds and sizes, reeds, grasses, etc.

Ikebana embraces the old as well as later, modified methods of flower arrangement. Even the primitive *rikkwa* method was understood as the 'putting of living flowers into vessels filled with water'. In *sunamono-rikkwa* the plants are put into boxes filled with sand. These structures, standing very high and broad, were set up in temple halls and temple gardens.

In the old pictures you can see drawings of mountains and foothills rising above one another to a point, and spreading out below to form a triangle.

The Technique

This mountainous landscape is intersected by valleys which stand out as empty spaces. Such models were meant to serve as eye-lines and points of departure in practical work. In the course of time the overloading that can be seen in the old models was simplified and clarified. The form of the triangle was emphasized more and more plainly and was retained as the basic pattern.

The later methods of flower arrangement can be distinguished as follows:

1. *Seikwa* (pronounced 'seika'). This implies the idea of cut flowers, and has the same meaning as *ikebana*. The word *seikwa* is derived from the Chinese word for *ikebana*.

2. *Nageire*. The 'loose' way of arranging flowers.

3. *Moribana*. Gives the picture of a landscape.

The symbolic Principle of Three is basic to all three methods.

SEIKWA

Seikwa falls into three kinds, for the triangle can be shifted about elastically. We distinguish between the formal, the semi-formal, and the informal

Plum (*ume*)

Formal, ceremonial *seikwa* showing five branches with plum
blossom in severe, very erect attitude

method. (Such a division into three is used in the Japanese and Chinese styles of writing and painting, as well as in the lay-out of gardens.)

Formal *seikwa* is also called classical *seikwa,* because it looks severe, serious, even solemn. The lines are vertical, pointing up to heaven. This ceremonial, almost stiff method of arranging flowers, their front side usually facing the altar, was used for decorating the altars of temples and ancestral shrines. Although this form is considered old-fashioned, it can still be seen on religious occasions today.

Semi-formal *seikwa* is particularly suitable for the rooms of dwelling-houses. In every house flowers find a worthy frame in the *tokonoma.* There the moderate, everyday form of *seikwa* has the best chance of spreading out comfortably to either side.

Informal *seikwa,* in its glorious attire, is said to resemble an elegant lady in wonderful negligée. This relaxed, imaginative form has various lines at its disposal. It can embellish a home either in the *tokonoma,* or on dainty lacquer stands, or in hanging containers. It is graceful and composed at once.

In *shin-seikwa* as in formal *seikwa* the accent is on the strong predominance *shin.* Like the drawn bow of a Japanese archer, it comes to stand almost vertical, in a high, wide curve. According to the peculiarity of the plants used, the branches, thick or slender as the case may be, will be shaped upwards in a strong or delicate arch.

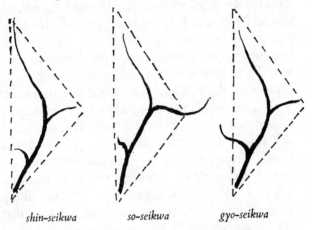

shin-seikwa   so-seikwa   gyo-seikwa

So-seikwa is characterized by a more informal-looking style, flowing and imaginative, like a piece of Japanese calligraphy. Here again the important thing is the shaping. *So* should spread out laterally, as if following its natural bent, and contrast strongly with the other branches.

Gyo-seikwa has a more restrained and compact structure. Generally it has a simple, squat, stumpy effect, looking as if it were rooted there. In all these settings the lower branches must be joined firmly together in order to give the stems a clear outline.

After cutting the Y-shaped fork and fixing it in the vase, the pupil will examine the material before him and mentally bring it into line with the basic pattern. Only then will he try to arrange the branches, paying attention to the peculiarity of each. In order to emphasize the three main lines, he will begin with them. There is no rigid rule about the sequence in which the branches should be arranged, as there is so much variety that a different treatment will be called for each time. Priority is often given to *so*, because it expresses the mid-point between heaven and earth, and the other two main branches can be added on to it, together with the subsidiary lines. The arrangement of the main branches that act as supports, and of the subsidiary lines that serve for decoration and filling up gaps, is shown on the opposite page.

In spring and summer the picture will be a rich and joyful one, in winter it will be rather more frugal but no less charming for that. In building it up, the pupil must take care that no branch hides the other and that they do not overlap. Each branch should be given the chance to spread out freely, its

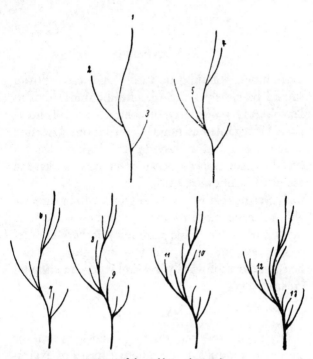

Names of the Additional Branches

1. Heaven (*shin*), top branch.
2. Man (*so*), middle branch.
3. Earth (*gyo*), low ranch
4. Rear Supplement to Heaven (*shin-ura-no-soe*)
5. Middle stem support (*do* or *daki*)
6. Supplement to Heaven (*shin-no-soe*)
7. Supplement to Earth (*gyo-no-soe*)
8. Extra Supplement to Heaven (*shin-no-soe*)
9. Shoot (*susho*)
10. Rear Supplement to Heaven (*shin-ura-no-soe*)
11. Extra Supplement to Man (*so-no-soe*)
12. Extra Supplement to Man (*so-no-soe*)
13. Extra Supplement to Earth, also called rear branch (*gyo-no-soe* or *oku-eda*).

extremities pointing upwards, and each flower should be clearly visible despite the number of its leaves. Any uniformity of contrasts would, however, be regarded as mindless repetition. Attention should be given to asymmetry and to leaving certain places open, because 'emptiness' has an essential significance.

Nevertheless the advanced pupil will, in time, be able to leave more room for a certain amount of individuality. The basic pattern is not there in order to suppress, but to help him to grow on to it, so that he can become inwardly free and independent in his creative acts.

NAGEIRE

In *nageire* too the three ground-lines can be shifted and moulded into different forms of expression. These trends can be suggested easily enough within the framework of an upright, dipping, or hanging style.

In the hanging form, the inclined branch or stem is also called the 'flowing' one, because it streams out yieldingly into its surroundings. Without use of a support, the branches or flowers dip down over the edge of the vase. As though lightly blown by the wind—so natural can the finished picture look.

Calla palustris (*kai-u*) and Scirpus lacustris *futo-i*
Aron lily and bulrush. *Moribana* with high water-level

The Technique

Often a single branch can bring the desired form in a quite unexpected way, but naturally the choice of material needs an expert eye. To shape a simple branch well is by far the hardest and is often a masterpiece.

The choice of containers is wide. For heavier branches one should use a bronze vase standing on a firm base, and porcelain for light, delicate flowers. Hanging containers or wall brackets are nicest for creeping plants with tendrils and for sideways-growing flowers. Plaited baskets, with handles that give support unnoticed, are also recommended.

Shitziho for Moribana Settings

MORIBANA

Moribana is arranged in shallow, very wide bowls of porcelain, stoneware, bronze, or lacquer. It

Salix (*yanangi*) Willow

Moribana landscape picture: willows in spring by the shore of
a lake in black lacquered container, silvered inside

allows the artist to create the effect of a segment of natural landscape. Various kinds of supports, made of heavy metal and called *shitziho*, can be combined as needed.

It is then left to the spectator's imagination to put himself into a certain mood, or into a certain landscape, by contemplating a few bulrushes or reeds, a water-lily or two, or some land-flowers standing by the water.

For summer, a large quantity of water will give life to segment of landscape. For winter, land occupies the foreground. The interplay of plants and water creates the impression of an inland region by a lake or river. The scene may reflect a woody, mountainous or marshy landscape, or it may look like an island or a river bank. By suggesting little trees, bushes, or undergrowth you can build up the effect of the triangle, with foreground, middle distance, background. Harmonious balance is achieved by the wealth of contrasts and the variegated arrangement. A tall branch can suggest, very simply, a 'tree' in the background. For the middle distance, you should use something bushy to represent woods or undergrowth. Short stalks, flat-growing plants, and moss are suitable for the foreground. For autumn scenes, you might consider a

Moribana
Old pine trunk on rough river-bank, with three boulders in
foreground

leaflesss 'tree' or branch, with berries in front of it, or grasses to suggest the bank of a river.

Much prized are small branches covered with the mossy patina of age, and adorned with fresh shoots in the spring. (These, naturally, must be arranged in such a way that they look as if they were growing out of the stem.) Mountains and rock can be indicated in the form of stones. If you want to indicate land shelving into water, this can be done with low plants, moss, small bulrushes, a sprinkling of stones. A stone lying in the water can suggest cliffs washed by the sea.

If three stones are used, the upright one on the right stands for the masculine *yo*-principle (*yang* in Chinese), and one of the smaller ones for the feminine *yin*-principle. This arrangement is borrowed from the Chinese and has found its way into various definitions and applications of art.

Yo signifies the sunny side, the front side that is turned towards the spectator. Erect, bright, strong, active, creative, it symbolizes the generative, flowering principle of Nature. Its colours are red, purple, pink.

Yin, on the other hand, is receptive. It is thought of as dark, lying in the shadow. Its form, less developed than that of *yo*, is suggested by buds and

Moribana
arundinaria phragmilis (reed)
Boats moored by the shore

curves. It is correlated with the left side, and its colours are white, yellow, blue.

The *yo-yin* classification is not intended to demonstrate a contrast, but rather a principle of balance and complementarity.

Hence, in using the three stones, the tall, powerful one would stand for elevation, 'heaven', the horizontal, lower one for 'man', while a flat stone added to create balance would symbolize 'earth'. Man, therefore, is situated between two powers, the bright and the dark. This is also the position assigned to him in the basic pattern of flower arrangement.

Since there are countless possibilities of expression in *moribana*, great care must be taken to create an effect of unity. For instance, land and water plants should not as a rule be used together in the same bowl.

Moribana has many ways of giving life to flower compositions and enabling us to feel the presence of Nature even in a closed room.

THE FLOWERS' WAY

THE TEN VIRTUES

AN OLD tradition lists the ten virtues which the flower Master must make his own if he wants to penetrate into the spirit of the 'true teaching', and which he at the same time acquires once he has penetrated into it. In quite simple words something is said that at first sight looks insignificant, indeed childish. But here, as so often in the Far East one, must know how to read between the lines.

1. Flower-setting brings high and low into spiritual relationship.
2. Carry 'Nothing' in the heart. It is 'Everything'.
3. Quiet, clear feeling. You can reach solutions without thinking.
4. Freedom from all cares.
5. Intimate, sensitive relationships with plants and the essence of Nature.
6. Love and esteem all men.

7. Fill the room with harmony and reverence.
8. 'True spirit' nourishes life; combine flower arrangement with religious feeling.
9. Harmony of body and soul.
10. Self-denial and reserve; freedom from evil.

Only one who has lived for a long time in the East knows that by 'freedom from all cares' is meant the capacity to accept with composure even the most merciless blows of fate. The frequent cataclysms of nature in Japan demonstrate that even among quite simple people there is an astounding spiritual strength behind this saying.

Similarly, the 'intimate relationship with nature' is not a mere phrase and means very much more than this simple expression would suggest. For instance, at the festival of the cherry blossom no blossoms are picked from the trees by the enthusiastic spectators, not even from trees with low-hanging branches. And in every coolie you can observe what a delicate understanding he has of flowers, how genuinely and unaffectedly his love of nature expresses itself. Seldom does anyone pick flowers on a walk. He likes best to leave them where they grow. Hardly ever are they picked in the woods and fields by children, let alone lost on the way.

Pinus (*matsu*) Pine

Pine *seikwa* growing naturally on a single branch, and shaped
into the three main lines, in suitable bronze vase

Anyone who has insight into Japanese ink-painting knows that 'intimate relationship with plants' means more than a sentimental love of Nature. What is meant is a productive relationship which discovers the essence of things, sees as it were into their hearts. Carrying 'Nothing' in the heart means possessing the highest and ultimate— 'Everything', the universe itself. To be close to this essence of the universe, to be able to live from it, from this original nature of the heart, creates that 'true spirit' which 'nourishes life'. And equally, one who is familiar with the 'essence of Nature' will also understand the essence of man, and 'love and esteem' him for the sake of the 'true spirit' which can come alive in him. An example of this is the readiness of the Japanese to help one another during natural catastrophes.

It is evident, then, that the ten virtues are not nearly so innocuous as they appear at first sight. Properly understood, they represent a rigorous disciplining of the mind. Anyone who has passed through this, functions in such a deep way that his activity, far removed from all mindless doing-for-its-own-sake, has its ground in the primal motion of the universe, which is one with the primal stillness.

In this connexion one is required to be 'empty

of oneself', to live in the 'harmony of body and soul' without petty, disturbing thoughts, to make room for the 'universal heart', and to be 'nothing and yet everything', carefree as a flower of the field.

These experiences come to expression in all Japanese arts. Therefore in flower arrangement the unfilled empty spaces are to be regarded as belonging to the total picture. They are just as important as the lines formed by the Principle of Three. They too manifest the inexpressible, irrepresentable, wordless silence. Rhythmically included in the unsymmetrical harmony, these empty spaces can be given particularly eloquent and clear expression. A most suggestive expression of silence is created by the quite unpretentious flower or plant, chosen for that very reason, which occupies a very important place in the tea-room, standing there with its mild colours and simple shape, as though it wanted to underline the significance of the tea ceremony and of the hour by its calm, self-contained silence.

In the immensity of emptiness everything condenses, finds its contrast, stands out in relief, as if reflecting in itself the infinite plastic power of the creative origin. In this way we enter into closer relationship with the unsymmetrical lines of the Principle of Three when we see them visibly taking shape in the living silence of space. In this union of emptiness and form the work outgrows its limitations and time-boundness. It lives as a new and free creation precisely by virtue of this continual formative power of emptiness.

In ink-painting, too, the empty spaces are included as a positive and meaningful, indeed indispensable, means of expression. What wide expanses are taken up by air, mist, cloud, and stretches of water barely hinted at! A Japanese proverb puts it very aptly: 'One painting is worth a thousand words'.

In the *Noh* plays and the old legends performed in the *Kabuki* theatre, the most striking and most significant passages are those where nothing is spoken at all, and the actor has to express everything wordlessly from within, by the most economical and yet concentrated mime and gestures.

In archery, the target is the 'empty Nothing' for the archer. The path of the arrow towards it springs from the discharge of highest tension. To be empty is to be one with all.

Haiku poetry, distinguished for its sparing use of words, reproduces the totality of an experience by the suggestive means of eloquent silence and concealment.

The First Requisite

Calligraphy actually requires a working together with empty spaces. Out of this emptiness speaks the 'form of the formless'; it expresses the 'content of the void', the 'image of the invisible'.

The tea-room bears the suggestive name: 'The Place of Emptiness'. It is only empty, all-embracing space that makes movement and concentration possible.

THE FIRST REQUISITE

Of the ten virtues, the first requisite is union with the 'flower heart' (*hana-no-kokoro*) and the 'universal heart'.

It is therefore quite natural that there must be no talking during the work and that any restlessness and fidgeting are prohibited. The reason for this lies not only in avoiding everything that might disturb or distract others in their concentration. Rather we see here the original meaning of flower arrangement as a religious ceremony. In keeping with this is the strict observance of cleanliness and order. For the room in which flowers are arranged may originally have been sacrosanct. This idea has been preserved to the present day. However plain and unassuming the room may be, it is consecrated by the flower arrangement if this is carried out in the 'true spirit'.

Thus the beginner is urged to be especially mindful of the 'flower heart'. Firstly in order to handle the flower correctly, secondly in order to live in the naturalness and security of his own heart. He should be like the flower heart, radiant, giving itself lavishly and yet at the same time serenely self-contained. And what he learns by listening to the flower heart and taking into his own heart, he communicates freely and without ulterior purpose to others. In this way a current of love runs from the flower heart to the human heart, to the universal heart and back again. It is this sacral and indescribable atmosphere that animates the room in which pupil and Master come together for a common task.

Intimately connected with the flower heart is the universal heart—the relationship with people. Yet all are equally important and equally justified. There is no preferred realm, say the realm of man and of human things, as if he were the crown of creation. There is not even a clearly delimited realm of life; for the Japanese all life is an uninterrupted unity, springing from a common root. If he distinguishes plants from animals and both from men, he nevertheless does not believe in differences of value, as though one were higher than the other, more important and more valuable in the meaning and purpose of its being. It may well be that a flower or a branch of blossom reflects the pattern of life more purely than the man who deems himself an exceptional phenomenon.

So anyone who believes that he can learn this art merely by showing himself sensitive to flowers and fairly tolerant in his dealings with animals is as ill-advised as the man who puts all the emphasis on the relationship with people, looking upon flowers and animals as more or less agreeable attendant phenomena which happen to be there 'too'. In his eyes they might not be there at all, and the realm of human life would suffer no loss! Flowers as a gratifying adornment, animals in the Zoo, these occasional encounters are sufficient for him, who has so many more important things to do. But in reality the study of flowers is just as important as the study of life itself in its variety, and the contact with men and animals is as important as that with flowers. The budding flower artist is not a specialist who can afford to neglect everything that is *not* flowers; rather, he relates himself to everything.

The relationship with plants may be granted a certain significance even in the life of a child. Generally a flower is the first 'live thing' that enters into his immediate circle. As soon as a plant is given into the charge of a child, the care he takes of it produces at the same time an inner relationship of protection and responsibility. Tending a plant and experiencing its growth also gives the child the task of watching over it lovingly. An instinctive sense of the connexion between human life and all Nature is awakened. It is an enrichment of the child's emotional life to observe the growth and development of plants. This sensitive understanding can then extend to the world of animals, to all Nature and the interrelationships in the cosmos.

With the child's observation of growth and development in Nature there comes a relationship to his own growth, a 'growing into' the sphere of his own tasks. Standing there so alive, the flower looks at everybody. Being together with flowers sensitizes the whole atmosphere. It is as though people could not behave meanly in the presence of flowers, and as though their nature were refined by having to do with them. There is no doubt that even a small bowl of flowers on the dining-table can alter a child's feelings, and that meals are quite different when eaten in barren surroundings. He even begins to cultivate a feeling of gratitude for what is received.

Another example might be mentioned here:

giving flowers to a sick person brings him new hope of recovery. Flowers on a grave testify to the eternal cycle of death and rebirth; they give solace and a promise.

No matter what the environment, flowers will impress their own stamp on it; they speak to us as if they were rooted in our lives. Even in a bare office, flowers on the desk can work wonders of relaxation and self-collection.

All this emphasizes the connexion and reciprocal action between men, plants, and the world. If, therefore, the pupil treads the 'flowers' way' aright, it will be clear to him from the beginning that the way does not lead into separate tracks. He is not guided only into outward, concrete, visible activity, for only silent communion with himself leaves him peaceful, relaxed, and devout enough to pass on to his work. From the centre of his being, from his inner self-collection, the way leads in a straight, harmonious line to the outer world. His eyes are filled with the wonder and beauty of the plants lying before him. Joined to the all-uniting being, taken up into the whole of the cosmos, he can create from the centre of his own humanity.

It may be that the pupil will look at the meaning of his task from two sides at first, until he is able to

Rhodea japonica (*omoto*)
Eleven-leaved *seikwa*, the fanwise arrangement of the light and
shadow sides creating a clear outline. The broad leaves shield
the red berries protectively

bring it to uniform expression. On the one hand he will develop quietness, patience and perseverance in his work. On the other, he will try to introduce as much as possible of this way of working into his practical life. Thus he does not stand still on the path, but can develop many-sidedly and find the middle way. He has given the flowers a new, living form and composition, and—without willing it—has put this form outside himself and inside himself simultaneously. This mutual interaction in the sense of the original teaching has seized his whole being, filled it, rounded it out. He lives in harmonious union with himself, his surroundings, and the universe. He is sustained by heaven as well as by the earth. And the natural way leads still further, beyond the symbolic handling of the flowers, the spouting water, the form-giving rocks. The pupil goes the 'flowers' way' not only in the isolated hour of practice or ceremonial. The living, creative presence of these hours will accompany him and lead him onward. The way can accompany life itself with ever new prospects and new beginnings. From this standpoint one can understand the saying that one treads this way 'as if not treading it', which means that way and pupil have become one.

The Flowers' Way

THE RIGHT ATTITUDE TO FLOWERS

There is a famous example of this: the story of a coolie who, struggling along a stony mountain path, discovered a thirsty flower, perishing with heat between the glowing boulders. Despite his load, he knelt down and poured his last drops of tea over the parched roots, so that the flower might survive the scorching heat. Then he hastened onward, unperturbed, to his distant goal. This story is not told for its strangeness, but because of its impressiveness.

Artists, too, have dealt with such motifs, for instance with that of the flowering convolvulus that wound itself round a well-rope during the night. It is related that a girl went out early one morning to draw water from the village well. But during the night a convolvulus had wound itself round the rope on which the bucket hung, and put forth a single blossom which opened its face to the light of day, drunk with joy. The girl, delighted and disconcerted at once, could not bring herself to disturb this wonderful happening. From a more distant well she carried back the filled buckets with joyful heart, paying no heed to the long detour.

A *haiku* poem commemorates it:

The Right Attitude to Flowers

> Round my well-rope
> Wound a convolvulus;
> Give me water, friend.

We ourselves once possessed a scroll painting on silk, showing this motif in a few suggestive lines. The little poem stood beside it.

It is related of the Chinese empress Komyo that she touched flowers only with reverence, thinking her hands might soil them: 'If I pluck you, flower, my hand would sully you'.

Such sensitivity characterizes the way of 'right behaviour', of delicacy towards one's surroundings. The more it is recognized and practised, the clearer it becomes that all this belongs to the requirements of flower-setting.

Observing them and sketching them from nature can make you so familiar with the life of the flowers that it is as if you had created them yourself.

Surrendering yourself with self-denial and patience, not making yourself important, adapting yourself gently, unobtrusively, without expecting thanks—all this is part of the flowers' way.

The gardener who, before each lesson, goes on request to the various lovers with a roll of straw matting under his arm, seems to fulfil something of

Iris ensata (*hana shobu*)

One of the many kinds of iris. *Seikwa* with eleven leaves
surrounding three flowers. Though *shin* forms the topmost
leaf, the accent is on the *gyo* line

these virtues. In it is a rich assortment of branches, blossom and flowers, tied together in bundles.

He has not chosen them at random, but carefully, thinking only of those which belong together. Nor would he dream of depriving the flowers of their leaves. Leaves and buds, as well as withered material, are all part of the complete replica of natural growth. With how much patience and friendly quietness he waits for the customer to make her choice! How cheaply he sells these flowery beings, and how modestly, carefully and becomingly he hands them to her!

Japan is known as the land of flowers. This must be understood in a quite special sense. In the gardens you find no flowers for cutting, but carefully protected and well-tended plants, bushes, and trees. They are looked after with great love and devotion, and the flowers are not willingly cut from the trees or shrubs. In the gardens you see plants that are arranged in curious patterns and ought not to be removed. Perhaps garden-grown flowers are the more valued because flowery meadows are hardly ever found. Apart from certain famous groves, to which people make reverent pilgrimages, free-growing flowers are something of a rarity. Gardeners have to grow the cut-flowers and sprays needed for the vases in the smallest space, as the rice fields take up most of the available land and every inch of ground must be used for food.

Yet at every season there are occasions for festive *o'hana-mi*, 'viewing the flowers'. Crowds of people, whole families, make pilgrimages to the famous beauty spots. There are the cherry orchards, stretching for miles and enchanting the eye. In the spring, shining white narcissi breathing sweetness in hidden valleys. Wistaria blossoms, hanging in lilac-coloured veils, vie with the scarlet of the Shinto buildings in ancient temple gardens. Long clusters of them festoon the bridges over which the marvelling sightseers cross. In the autumn, there are the flaming colours of the maple-woods, although the Japanese maple is equally attractive in the early spring, with its delicate red foliage, and in summer it is cool green.

The chrysanthemum (*kiku*) is the golden flower of the East and the heraldic flower. There are nearly two hundred varieties of this celebrated plant, whose cultivation is a joy to everyone, even the poorest. The chrysanthemum festival, which takes place every year on the 9th of September, is a national holiday.

There are iris and lotus lovers, and each of them knows where to find and admire his favourites.

Paeonia (*botan*) Tree peony

Informal, natural-grown *seikwa* with strong but natural
emphasis on *gyo*. In one of the favourite bamboo vases,
obtainable in all shapes and sizes

Thus, the peculiar understanding which the Japanese have for the art of flower arrangement is conditioned not least by their closeness to and love of Nature. It makes the symbolic language of the flowers intelligible to them and translates it, as it were, into visible presences.

The lotus, for instance, is regarded as the flower of religious worship. It is the symbol of purity and immortality. For it lifts itself, gazing heavenwards, up from the turbid water, from the muddy earth, in clear colours, surrounded by immaculately shining, bright-green leaves.

Buds and rolled-up leaves betoken the future. Full-blown flowers reveal the present. The seed-pods of flowers now withered speak of the past.

Plum blossom signifies resistance to injury and new hope. An old stem with young shoots on it means maturity coupled with tenderness. The peony, in its sumptuous glory, symbolizes splendour and riches. The pine stands for imperturbability, strength and firmness of character. Bamboo represents long life, durability, plenty, and so on.

Thus, besides the intrinsic nature of the flowers, what they say and express is also important. A comprehensive vision should be able to tell, from the way the flowers are arranged, what the finished product represents. A more refined vision can go a step further and read from the total picture the spiritual peculiarity of the artist, or more precisely, what stands behind it: the infinite, the inexpressible.

Ability to say everything in a few words, that was the secret of Bokuyo Takeda's mastery. A mellow life, rich in experience, gives one the creative power to do this.

In the course of the years it struck me that the younger the pupils were, the more brilliant were the flowers they chose for exhibiting. The beginner would like, for his own satisfaction, to see his vase placed in the foreground. More advanced pupils are content with the middle, while the bowl of the Master stands inconspicuously in the background. He is able to contrive such a skilfully balanced arrangement that his product makes a whole, a magnificent harmony of light and dark, loud and soft, brilliant and shadowy. So it is not surprising that these flower exhibitions are extraordinarily well visited. Not only the close relatives of those concerned, but the whole town takes part in this event. For there is no Japanese woman and hardly a Japanese man who does not have some connexion with the art of flowers and does not know what it signifies and what they owe it.

In spite of its delicacy, flower arrangement was originally practised by men, more particularly by those well tested by life. Self-immersion in union with the flowers breathes the very spirit of the samurai, and the gravity of final, irrevocable decisions.

Imagine what tremendous inner strength is expressed when the lord of a castle, which has already surrendered to the superior assaults of the enemy, still remains calm and composed enough to arrange flowers! This act may well be the last he will ever do, but it is not one of violence. It does not pretend to be anything special, it simply bears the stamp of something involuntary, of a true and detached life, of an art that is just as unartificial as the practice of 'true' archery.

Not only outwardly is the lord of the castle a knight, inwardly too he remains a victor not to be conquered by his foe. He is as unshakable in the face of death as he was in life. His being flows from the centre, which carries both heaven and earth, and is carried by both.

ART OR NATURE?

Can the finished product—the perfect form in which alone it unfolds its full essence—be considered

Paeonia (*botan*)
Nageire with three sprays. The hanging container of fine old
bronze represents the waxing moon

a work of art, even though of an art that subserves religious life and experience?

It is just the complete master of flower arrangement who is called upon to create works which look like the creations of Nature herself. Even though they are cut from the ground where they grew, it is nevertheless living flowers and branches of blossom that are put together to form a newly created unity, in which their nature is still preserved. For, in spite of all the bending and turning, the flowers and branches should not be twisted out of shape and distorted in a way that goes against their nature.

Now is such a flowerpiece a product of nature or of art? Or does it stand midway between the two, so that it is more than nature and not yet pure art? An unequivocal answer is extraordinarily difficult to give. For the Japanese, life and art, nature and spirit form an indissoluble unity, and unbroken whole. He experiences nature as having a soul, and spirit as part of nature, without purpose. So he cannot make sense of a question which presupposes a division of nature from spirit, life from art, as though they were alien to each other. For him nature is neither dead nor unspiritual, nor yet a mere symbol and semblance. The Eternal itself is

Patrinia scabiosaefolia (*ominaeshi*) Patrinia
Thirteen branches in graceful bronze vase with three feet

immediately present in its living beauty. This viewpoint is typical of all Japanese art. Consequently, we
fail to touch its real essence if we believe that it
'idealizes' its objects and aims at easing tensions
and reconciling opposites in order to create harmony. For the Japanese, harmony is the innermost
form underlying nature, life and the world, and art
can have no other task than to portray this harmony,
to confirm it through varying degrees of 'uncon-
scious awareness'. The artist will draw it into himself
as if with a deep breath from an infinite distance,
exalt it, and body it forth. With his senses wide
open, he perceives the new creation, and carries it
out of its background into visible form. Since he
gives up all thought of placing himself in the foreground, he will, simultaneously with the tangible
presence of the flower—in which the cosmos manifests itself—also become aware of the law of its
being, and of his own nature. He himself lives and
fashions his work from the 'formless Form'. The
artist combines in himself the creative impulse with
its realization, emptiness with fullness. Out of this
harmony beyond the opposites he lifts up his work
and carries it beyond itself.

This can be seen particularly clearly in the art of
flower arrangement. The true flower artist does not

pay so much attention to the outward form of nature, or to the form which is to be made visible only outwardly. For him the outward form is not the goal, but at best only a bridge leading to the inner form. It should please only in so far as it draws the eye inwards, to the depths where nature and spirit, life and ideal are one. The artist has the same relationship to the whole of nature which characterizes every Japanese who is not mis-educated, and which rests on his almost unbelievable capacity to see everything as a living totality.

Thus the choice of flowers and branches does not depend only on whether they harmonize with one another in arrangement and colour. It is far more important that they should be suitable for representing the inner form in which the artist experiences the world. Flowers, shrubs and trees satisfy this requirement, because they often have a symbolic meaning. The flower picture is expressive enough on account of the materials used. It says even more to the beholder through its combination of well-balanced and deliberated richness and simplicity, and also through the places that are left empty, mirroring concentration, strength, and modesty. To create such a whole thing, which despite its formality gives free play to the imagination and sets no bounds to experience—herein lies the 'artless art' of flower arrangement.

Yet not this art alone should be taught. Rather, as already emphasized, the Master is continually mindful that the pupil should realize with his entire being the 'unwritten teaching' until it becomes second nature to him, moulding his character until he can go the 'flowers' way' in his own life here and now. Then all groping ceases: the way has become living reality.

THE CEREMONY

THE FLOWER CEREMONY

THE FLOWER ceremony developed out of the same spiritual attitude as flower arrangement. It, too, by reason of its decidedly contemplative and symbolic character, points to the original connexion between flower arrangement and Buddhism.

The ceremony consists essentially in meditation and deep concentration, the prescribed rules referring only to its outward performance.

First of all, the guest has to contemplate the *kakemono* (written or painted scroll) hanging in the *tokonoma*. Then he absorbs himself in the flower-piece standing in the foreground. The host has matched the painting, which shows a mountain scene, with a branch of larch or a mountain flower. A lowland plant or flower would not be suitable for creating a complementary harmony; everything is done to assist the beholder as obligingly as possible.

The Ceremony

Next he has to turn his attention to the flower-piece itself, getting to know and understand it in all its details, beginning with the main branch.

This is the first part of the flower ceremony. Devout meditation and inconspicuous behaviour are expected of the beholder as a matter of course. The second part begins when the host invites his guest to arrange some flowers himself. The guest will modestly decline to accept his host's invitation, but on repeated requests he will finally consent. The host now gets everything ready. A few long-stemmed flowers or branches, easy to arrange, are laid in precise order on the flower board, together with the necessary containers, pruning-shears, and a cotton cloth. A little distance away is a can of water and a suitable vase on a stand.

The host retires with his other guests to an adjoining room and waits patiently until the chosen guest has arranged his flowers. He, meanwhile, is sunk in contemplation of the flowers, on bent knees, resting on his heels. Perhaps, in his thoughts, he is wandering in the fields where they grew—mountain country or flatland, by a river or by the sea. The *kakemono* in the wall-niche will help to complete his fantasy. An exquisite little figure or an incense burner, standing in the *tokonoma*, may like-

Prunus (*ume*) Plum
So–seikwa with special emphasis on *so*. Nine branches with
numerous blossoms, which appear before the leaves

wise strengthen the impression of harmony and lead to the completion of the work. The creative works harmoniously within and without. Not only immersion in the symbolism and nature of the flowers inspires the creator—he is filled and possessed by the essence of the things themselves. Pervaded by the warmth of the human heart, he gives expression to the universal heart.

Now the host calls the other guests and his family together, so that all can look at the finished work. The flower artist modestly resists at first, and begs his host to remove this unworthy product, without showing it. The host in his turn begs, with equal politeness, to be allowed to show this beautiful achievement to the others. And finally they all sit round the *kakemono* in a semicircle and compare it, appreciatively, with the flower-piece. Their faces reflect the beauty and harmony of the work; an inexpressibly serene atmosphere fills the room.

This flower ceremony is still occasionally practised today. Hardly in the big cities, of course, but only where Japanese life has still preserved its peculiar flavour.

The flower ceremony I have described helps one to understand that to talk of the 'true spirit' of flower arrangement is not just an empty phrase. For only so long as it is animated by this 'true spirit' can it fulfil the high task for which it was chosen.

It was from the 'true spirit' that this art sprang, and it should go on being cultivated in this spirit. Otherwise it will degenerate and become mere decoration, which no longer touches men's hearts.

RELIGIOUS ORIGIN

Branches from berry-bearing bushes have a symbolic meaning. When, in old age, a man gives up his profession in order to devote himself to another kind of life, this transition is symbolized by berry-bearing branches. They are meant to indicate how a life of another kind, dedicated to philosophy or philanthropy or art, is not idle, but can bear much fruit.

Tradition tells us of Indian monks who, in their universal love, were the first to pick up plants injured by the storm or parched by the heat, in order to tend them with compassion and endeavour to keep them alive. In the chambers of Buddhist temples miniature gardens in heavy bronze vessels, and boxes filled with sand, were placed before the image. In these, room could be made for plants and branches of the most various kinds, including heavy boughs and even stumps of trees.

The central, highest branch pointed straight up to heaven. To the left and right, more branches were grouped round the lower, subsidiary centres, in a vertical, symmetrical arrangement. A third group, the 'auxiliaries', had the task of supporting and holding the whole together. In the old pictures you can see such groupings arranged symmetrically on either side of the altar. This early way of arranging plants, which the monks placed in the temples, temple gardens, and also before graves, as sacrificial and honorary gifts, was known in Japan under the names *shin-no-hana, rikkwa, sunamono-rikkwa,* and *bukkwa.*

Out of these vertical, rather overloaded arrangements there developed in the course of time quite new compositions, smaller in scale and with more elegant, simpler lines, that looked typically Japanese. This happened in the fifth century, when Buddhism entered Japan through Korea, and Chinese priests introduced many new customs along with this teaching. In addition to their religious function, the Buddhist temples became seats of learning, where philosophy, poetry, calligraphy, painting and other arts were fostered. Thus the monastic way of life

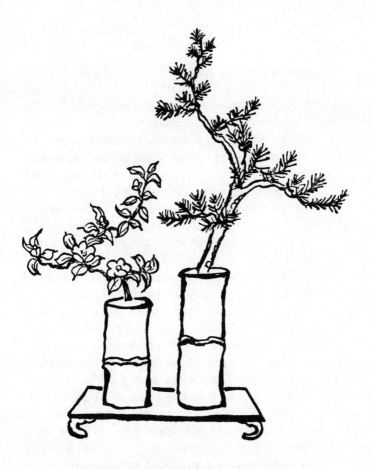

Wedding Decoration

Two vases of plain bamboo tied with a coloured cord (*mizu-hiki*) as a sign of lasting union. The gnarled pine branches in the taller vase are a masculine symbol, and the white camellia symbolizes gentle femininity. The flower should not look at the beholder full face, nor should it be hidden by leaves, but should be set somewhat obliquely

came into living relationship with artistic creation.

The ritual of tea drinking was also first practised in the Zen monasteries, and it was there too that the ceremony of incense-burning originated.

So it was mostly monastically trained adepts who produced famous works of art in connexion with the tea ceremony that grew up at the end of the fourteenth and fifteenth centuries. Together with the tea cult and the introduction of the *tokonoma,* they fostered the flower cult in its characteristic form and became at the same time great flower Masters.

They also gave their attention to the lay-out of gardens. It was considered that the lines and relationships between the inside and outside of a room should balance and contrast with one another to form a complementary whole. For the wide sliding doors remain open during the day on the garden or park side, so that there is hardly any interruption between the room and its view.

Thus garden culture underwent new developments thanks to the many-sided gifts of these Masters. Their creative talents passed into the stock of Japanese culture. Modelled on the severe, strictly disciplined simplicity of the Zen monasteries and their surroundings, the tea rooms added on to the

Camellia (*tsubaki*)

Nageire with supplement (*nejime*) of willow branches in plaited basket-vase. The container is attached to a pillar of rare wood, polished smooth and shiny by daily use

house or set up in the gardens of private houses and palaces were built in monastic style. Its impressive, clean lines had an influence on Japanese architecture in general.

Into this combination of ritual and sensitive feeling, which characterizes the tea-room, the living plant could be introduced only with the utmost simplicity and naturalness. Often nothing more stood there than a small, exquisitely-shaped branch, or a flower surrounded by tender green leaves. Preferably the plant was stood in a quite unpretentious-looking container of plain bamboo or bark, or in a gourd, which was suspended from one of the pillars of rare wood supporting the little, very neatly kept tea-room. This kind of fixture favoured hanging plants and field flowers, and anything that grew wild.

This supremely natural yet very choice way of arranging flowers is called *nageire*, meaning 'to put in, throw in', with reference to the naturalness and easy nonchalance with which they hang down over the edge of the vase. Yet the melody of the triple rhythm can still be perceived through the un-symmetrical silhouette. Contrasting with this most natural mode of flower arrangement, altogether new and different possibilities developed for the specially large room in which guests were received and in which the *tokonoma*—the worldly counterpart of the original altar—began to take the place of honour.

In a rhythm adapted to the events of the day, whether social gatherings or festivals, flowers were arranged, in order to give these the honour and respect due to them. Thus, according to the occasion, the flowers could share in the rejoicings in a splendid array of glowing colours and forms, or could bear witness to the dignity of quiet simplicity.

The great variety of amateur practitioners and festive occasions demanded from the leading Masters an especially fine feeling for form and for methods of instruction. Thus it came about quite naturally that different schools and trends developed, with definite rules and exceptions. Yet they almost always remained faithful to the original idea of the three main lines as the foundation of art and experience. In the sixteenth and particularly the seventeenth century this kind of flower arrangement reached its climax. Priests, scholars, poets, nobles as well as men who had given up their professions and withdrawn from the worries and bustle of everyday life, became enthusiastic adherents of this wonderful form of self-communion.

The word *ikebana*, which means putting living

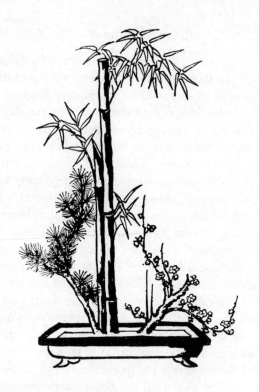

New Year's Decoration

Bamboo (*take*), symbol of plenty, resilience, riches; pine (*matsu*), symbol of endurance and strength; plum (*ume*), symbol of new hope after winter. Young shoots are sometimes added to an old stem. Each of the plants exhibits individually and in the composition as a whole the division into three. The decoration can be set up over the door as well as in the room itself, either in one or in three containers. If two bamboos are used, the shorter is the feminine and the taller the masculine symbol

plants in water, pledges one to love the flowers as living things and to tend them with kindly feelings. Even the water you give them should be poured out with the consciousness that you are responsible for the life of the flower. This explains why the New Year's decorations, bringing good fortune and consisting of pine, plum and bamboo set before the door of the house, may not be thoughtlessly thrown away after the New Year's week is over. Instead, all these flower-pieces are carried to the temple on a certain evening, piled up and burnt. The crackling flames leap up and illuminate the old temple and the dark Japanese cedars, round which thousands of spectators have gathered.

According to an old legend, symbolic flower arrangement was of divine origin. A supernatural being, Fudo-dama-no-mikoto by name, planted the *sakaki*, the tree sacred to Shintoism, in honour of the sun goddess Amaterasu o-mi-Kami.

Maybe this tradition contains the subsidiary idea that the art of flower arrangement was originally Japanese. Strictly speaking, this view is not quite correct. It is true only in so far as the Japanese took over the primitive impulse that was imported into their country and developed it independently into a high and typically Japanese art.

The Ceremony

Although flower arrangement became, in the course of time, a secular art, it never lost that mysterious quality it acquired from its original association with religious ceremonial. The Japanese will still bow, sometimes, before the flowers he has arranged. He will also bow to the work of others before examining it, and again before taking his departure after thorough examination.

THE TEA CEREMONY

Wood and meadow flowers are particularly suitable for the room in which the tea ceremony is held, and where—to avoid distraction—absolute simplicity reigns. The presence of these ingenuous little flowers can be very affecting, especially in the extremely modest and yet exquisite room which is expressly designed for the tea ceremony.

It may be a single flower, heightening the sanctity of the tea room by its living presence; yet it will not attract attention to itself by smelling strongly, or by brilliant colours. On the contrary! Perhaps all you can see are the demure outlines of a small convolvulus with delicate pink buds. The flower also symbolizes the attitude of mind that is expected here. From a bamboo container, affixed to the rare wood of the

Wall niche (*tokonoma*)

Lily in hanging horn container, attached to a pillar of rare wood, polished smooth with age, in the corner of the *tokonoma*. In the foreground, an incense burner

pillar flanking the *tokonoma*, it gazes dreamily and musingly towards the entrance door. There, through the low opening of the hallway, come the few guests invited to the tea ceremony. Bowing modestly, they slowly make their way in. First they have carefully washed their hands at the fountain outside, before leaving behind them, on the moss-bordered paving-stones, their shoes together with the outside world. Stillness, peace, and the gleam of cleanliness pervade this muted inner room. A soft wind blows, from far away in the bamboo groves. It passes over the charcoal brazier let into the floor, on which the tea-kettle stands. The guests listen to the soft, metallic simmering of the bubbling water. Perhaps the strong green powdered tea will be beaten into a froth with a very small bamboo whisk, or perhaps black tea is being prepared in the elabo-rately ceremonious manner.

For a long time the guests sit, modestly expectant, in their characteristic attitude, letting the ceremonial action of tea-making, each movement of which is prescribed, slowly run its course. To perform this art quietly and composedly requires a kind of hieratic attitude, which silently communicates itself to those present. All the implements used are dis-tinguished for their simplicity and good taste. Often they are family heirlooms. From the pillar by the wall, the convolvulus looks on, sharing everything. It was watered before the ceremony began. When the guests are handed their cup of tea in turn, and sip the drink slowly and meditatively, then it too will not need to feel thirsty.

THE CEREMONY OF INCENSE BURNING

The burning of the incense sticks is an impressive ceremony. The scroll of calligraphy hanging in the *tokonoma*, and specially chosen for the purpose, is designed to reflect the seriousness and spirituality of the hour. This calligraphic art, written by the monkish hand of a Master, still lives and breathes. A scroll of this sort has the power in it to reawaken the spirit out of which it was originally created. It symbolizes the disciplined simplicity of the outer and inner form and guides the beholder's thoughts back to the religious rites in the sanctuary.

The essence of the word *sesshin* (strict spiritual discipline, collecting one's thoughts) reigns in this room.

The budding flower, surrounded only by a few leaves, takes part in the quiet seriousness of its surroundings. It does not compete either with the strange perfume of the burning incense stick, nor with the exotic shape of the venerable incense container that stands in the middle of the *tokonoma*.

Self-obliviously, it lets the clouds of incense roll round it and the solemn hour pass by, as if it knew that its scent were less important than the immediate presence of its wonderfully created form.

THE FLOWERS AND THE GUEST

In this hospitable country, one of the first considerations when building a house is the place which is always kept ready for the honoured guest. Another consideration is the flowers, for which a special place must be reserved too. For the guest is reserved the nicest corner of the room, in front of the *tokonoma*; for the flower, the lower elevation of the *tokonoma* itself. In the very large room that serves as a reception room, usually two scrolls hang on the wall, complementing one another in meaning. These *kakemonos* are pictures painted in ink on silk or thin paper, unframed, but mostly edged with brocade. The scroll may also contain a piece of calligraphy, executed by the hand of a Master, and reproducing a short but profound thought.

If there are two *kakemonos* hanging on the wall,

Peony (*botan*)
Informal *seikwa* with strong emphasis on *gyo*

the flower-piece should stand in the middle, to the front of the *tokonoma*. In especially large and solemn rooms there may be three scrolls, depicting a consistent motif. Here, by way of exception, there should be two flower-pieces. In some houses there are two rooms, each with a *tokonoma,* and in this way it is possible to enliven several rooms with flowers in large vases. The guest will approach these flowers at a becoming distance; near them he will find some object in lacquer, bronze or porcelain, valued by its owner, or some other work of art. Occasionally such an object will attract the eye by its choice simplicity. Only among good friends are these things looked at closely and perhaps submitted to examination. These loved and respected treasures, long guarded, are only brought out one at a time, because each of them needs appreciating on its own. Perhaps it will be taken out of one of the numerous chests and unwrapped only as a special mark of honour to the expected guest. The treasure is not displayed in an ostentatious manner. At such meetings the flower-piece sets the tone and may serve as a prelude to further examination.

The lady of the house or some member of the family takes time off to arrange the flowers for her own inner harmony and at the same time to delight others and show them honour. When a guest is expected, the flowers are once more sprinkled with water. They must look dewy fresh when they greet him on his arrival.

Generally a single, well-chosen and well-formed flower-piece is sufficient for restful contemplation. Hardly ever more than a hanging container with set flowers is put in the same room with it.

The eye of the guest may, on arrival, be attracted to the words conjured on to the scroll in symbolic writing. Since this kind of *kakemono* merits special attention, careful thought must be given to the choice of an appropriate flower. Great importance is attached to the high art of calligraphy, to the rhythmic movement of the verbal images in conjunction with the empty spaces. The 'content of the void' will fill the spectator, as also will the style of writing and the meaning of the words, which can often be taken in two ways.

Sometimes considerable intuition and knowledge are needed in order to grasp the meaning quickly. Yet such a picture needs to be appreciated in its whole expression without too much intellectual analysis, and to be looked at again and again. The total vision out of which the artist formed it should draw the spectator under its spell; it is the harmony

Nageire
Composed of different autumn flowers, loosely set and
inclining to one side, in moon-vase

of the inner content with its outward form. There are innumerable *haikus* which can describe a particular mood in very few words. By limiting the number of words and the means of expression, the imagination of the observer is brought into play.

Thus, for instance, there are countless *haikus* on the full moon and the waxing moon. A fitting complement to the 'moon released by clouds' might be clear water framed by a silver bowl or in a bowl of night-black lacquer. The moon in the accompanying picture should be reflected in the transparency of the still water.

Similarly, there are poems singing of the coloured maple leaves scattered by the autumn. The picture shows them carried away by the wind in glowing colours, which are caught in a shallow bowl.

Another scroll, written in loose calligraphy with much space in between, might tell of an old samurai or priest, and of the sublime composure with which he met his death. The accompaniment to this would be a few scattered cherry blossom petals, as if wafted across still water by the spring wind.

Perhaps a present is to be given to the honoured guest. It is handed to him in a little box made of wonderfully light *kirin* wood, or in a carton wrapped in special gift paper and tied with the usual red and white string. Even when the gift consists of blossoms in bud, they are tied lightly together and swathed in a ceremonial gift wrapping. Even the simplest person will comply with this custom. The gift may have no material value, but he will not fail to hand it over solemnly wrapped up. Here I cannot help thinking of our two good rickshaw boys, who, after receiving a New Year's present, responded with due decorum. Their gift consisted of bamboo chopsticks which they had made themselves. Ceremoniously, in just such a wrapping, they were handed over, a friendly response from man to man.

THE SUBSTANCE OF THE TEACHING

When one studies the 'true teaching', one becomes more clearly aware of the characteristically Oriental conception of freedom. In the East, inner freedom is understood to mean adapting yourself to forms which have the significance of cosmic laws. By adapting himself to them, the pupil takes his place in a coherent world order. The triadic pattern that underlies flower-setting is nothing less than a cosmic principle. Only by adapting himself to this principle can the floral artist reach the solid ground where his creative powers can develop to the full. He is then free to depict the schematic relationships in a living way. Neither mindless imitation of this schema, nor a misplaced originality that thrusts it aside unthinkingly, would be the right thing. Both would be looked upon as a transgression against the 'true teaching' and the spirit of flower-setting.

Hence, as repeatedly emphasized, inner discipline, adaptability and the capacity for self-denial are demanded of the pupil. On these qualities, which become more and more self-evident, the teacher sets the greatest value from the beginning; they seem to him more important than a light, skilful hand or good taste.

Although self-renunciation and dissolution in the spiritual principle of the world are regarded in the East as the highest good and constitute the deepest meaning of life, this does not mean that a work born of such an attitude must be completely impersonal. Even the Eastern artist cannot prevent his work from showing traces of individuality—indeed, this is an essential part of it—yet his individuality should not disturb the spirit of the work but must be fully absorbed by it. This means that the artist should not make a deliberate attempt to give his work a personal note. Only so far as this streams into the work unintentionally and fuses spontaneously with the law of its being in perfect unity, is it justified and even has a profound meaning.

What we see here, in the modest domain of flower arrangement, is characteristic of all Eastern art and particularly of the Zen-Buddhist outlook on life. Everything ultimately depends on what is outside and beyond the opposites, on the spirit, and on man's capacity not only to dissolve himself in it through passionate self-immersion, but also to live out of it with equal composure. This is not a negation or a flight from the world.

From whatever side the Westerner seeks access to the spiritual life of the East, he will encounter quite special difficulties. Almost always he is in danger of wanting to penetrate intellectually into what lies beyond the intellect, into something that is given to Eastern man directly, and which he experiences in unquestioning reality. The difficulty of coming to an intellectual understanding is further exacerbated by the fact that the Oriental seldom feels any desire to explain his experience in intellectual terms. Consequently, there is often a deep gulf between what he says with words and what he really means by them. Mostly he has to content himself with bare hints and images, if he does not take refuge in paradox. To find the right approach and *not* regard understanding of what the teacher says as understanding of the thing itself, demands much intuitive patience from the Westerner, and constantly renewed attempts somehow to guess and experience what it is all about. Even though there are many things in flower-setting that can be said and shown, yet behind everything that can be visibly represented there stands, waiting to be experienced by everyone, the mystery and deep ground of existence.

It should be evident from what has been said that flower arrangement is concerned with this inner, spiritual principle. But one must be quite clear that the right attitude has nothing to do with mood.

That which underlies this art and needs to be experienced is in itself formless, but it takes on form as soon as you try to represent it symbolically. And it is just this spiritual form that constitutes the essence of flower arrangement. By adhering strictly to the cosmic pattern, the artist learns, in accordance with the Eastern attitude of pure, unpurposing surrender to the laws of the cosmos, to experience them through and through. At the same time he breaks through to the depths of his own being, which rests on those same laws.

Here without doubt is the key to an understanding of Eastern art and the spiritual life of the East in general: in this 'looking away from oneself', in the utter 'unpurposingness' of its highest spiritual achievements. Thus the painter brushes his strokes not as though *he* painted them, but as though they painted themselves from the primal 'Ground'. Thus, too, the flowers are not brought into harmony by looking at them first from one side and then from the other, by experimenting and comparing—only the beginner does that—rather, the eye is directed inwards. Not the slightest intention of arranging them 'beautifully' must disturb this self-immersion, not even the desire to become 'purposeless on purpose'. If you succeed in producing this frame of

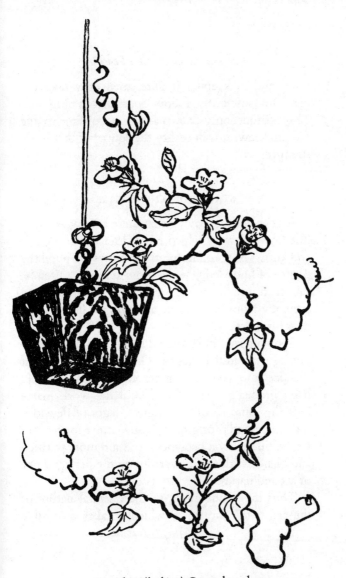

Cucurbita (*hechima*) Cucumber plant

Nageire with 'flowing' tendril of cucumber plant surrounding
a suspended wooden vessel representing bucket and well-rope

mind and in keeping it pure, then only does the hand unconsciously follow spontaneous impulses. This attitude only *looks* passive; according to the Eastern view, it is in reality the source of that inner strength.

STAGES OF KNOWLEDGE

It goes without saying that there are stages along 'the flowers' way' which the Master can recognize and knows how to interpret. He shows the pupil the degree of knowledge he has now attained. Often he can read the beginner's character with uncanny accuracy from the way he arranges his flowers and does his work.

Spontaneity and individuality seldom appear during the initial stages. Only through patient practice and continual inner transformation does habit gradually wear away, until the work manifests the 'pure form'. At higher stages of development the pupil's 'originality' can venture forth more freely, till finally it becomes more and more purified and blends with the 'pure truth' in the perfect unity of art and nature.

Thus the 'truth' finds, in the essential nature of the artist, the theatre in which it takes on visible

Chrysanthemum (*kiku*)
Seikwa with seven flowers and two buds in basket-vase

form. To embody the truth of 'Heaven itself'—this is the highest task, whose solution is granted only to the best poets and painters. And if he is successful, the flower artist will find it rising out of himself with unforced naturalness, like a gift that can never be lost.

Yet behind the visible forms there is always the form that cannot be expressed and cannot be represented, the eternal mystery, which he struggles in vain to apprehend, unless it reveal itself unhoped for.